THE
RETIREMENT
SUCCESS
Solution

Advantage
PERSONAL FINANCE™

E. RONALD LARA, CFP

The Retirement Success Solution™ by Ron Lara
© 2006 by E. Ronald Lara, CFP
All Rights reserved.
ISBN: 1-59755-091-4

Published by: ADVANTAGE BOOKS™
www.advbooks.com

Library of Congress Control Number: 2006925990

First Printing: April 2006
04 05 06 07 08 09 10   9 8 7 6 5 4 3 2 1
Printed in the United States of America

Acknowledgements

I wish to thank my lovely wife Patrice for all her help in the writing of this book.

My Coach2 friends for their encouragement. Mark Yontz and Robert Stuberg for their assistance and guidance. Gil Smith for his suggestions. All of my clients for their trust and confidence over the past 35 years of my career.

Table of Contents

Author Bio

E. Ronald Lara, CFP.

With more than 35 years of financial planning experience, Ron has reached a point in his successful career where he now works primarily with high net-worth clients. He has become an expert on helping clients plan for their retirement goals and needs, all while using a philosophy that revolves around staying active and, instead of retiring "cold turkey," spending time doing what you enjoy and delegating (or eliminating) everything else. His philosophy of determining the growth rate needed to achieve your retirement goals, as well as your lifetime goals, has enabled his clients to retire using a more conservative approach to investing then was previously thought possible.

A native of the Washington, D.C. area, Ron's interests and goals led him to the University of Maryland, where he graduated in 1968 with a bachelor of science in civil engineering. Ron worked for Humble Oil and Refining Company for a year before serving in the United States Army through April 1971.

Following his military service, Ron entered the financial services field and in 1977 he became one of the first designated Certified Financial Planners (CFP) in the Washington, D.C. area. He then started his own firm, Lara, Shull & May, Ltd., in 1981.

During the mid-80's, in an on-going attempt to maximize the investing power of his clients, Ron developed a strategy for purchasing US Treasury bonds, which prompted him in 1987 to formally start his Treasury Bond Management program. After the success of this program, The Lara Group was formed in 1991 for the sole purpose of managing U.S. Treasury Bonds.

Today, Ron continues to serve as president of Lara, Shull & May, Ltd., a Vienna, Virginia and Frisco, Colorado-based financial services planning firm that provides clients with a full range of investment, financial planning and specialized estate planning services. The firm has also developed, and offers, a set of helpful, proprietary online tools for investors. This includes The Lifetime Success Solution®, which is a comprehensive financial planning process that helps clients achieve both financial and lifetime goals.

On a more personal side, Ron's many charitable affiliations included memberships on the board of directors for The Fairfax Library Foundation, The Claude Moore Colonial Farm at Turkey Run, and Joe Gibbs' Youth for Tomorrow. A devoted family man, Ron is married with five children and his hobbies include skiing, flying, tennis and attempting to play golf.

INTRODUCTION

There's no way around it: Planning for retirement is a vitally important step, as your ability to enjoy living following a life's worth of work depends upon it.

However, preparing for retirement can be marred by all kinds of obstacles and pitfalls, many of which are related to the actual process of saving the money needed to retire comfortably. Does it always have to be this way? Absolutely not, because there are things you can do (and need to do now) to make sure you have the financial resources necessary at your disposal when they are needed most.

For 35 years, I have been working with clients, helping them develop and implement effective tax, savings and investment strategies. Early on in my career, my only concern was offering people investment plans designed to outpace inflation and provide some long-term growth. In the early '70s no one had heard of asset allocation. In short, the main idea was dollar cost averaging, which is the systematic investment of a specific dollar amount each month. For those individuals who invested in this manner, it lowered their average cost and rewarded them with impressive double-digit returns over the next thirty years.

But as I worked more with older clients, people who were nearing or already at retirement age, I began to see they needed to move their investment efforts beyond the dollar cost averaging approach that was so popular during the '70s and '80s.

Throughout my career, financial-related forces – such as inflation, rising and falling interest rates, and rising/declining stock markets – have consistently made making a positive return on your investment a difficult proposition. For example, during the early '80s high interest rates brought heavenly returns if you invested in fixed income investments, such as government bonds, municipal bonds and mortgage-backed bonds. Case in point, during the early '80s government-backed Ginnie Mae bond yields peaked at 17 percent and money market funds yielded in excess of 20 percent, which is quite a contrast to the barely 1 percent yield on money market funds in early 2004. Keep in mind, however, the high inflation rates that came along with this period acted as a negative, long-term counterbalance to the money people thought they were making in these safe investment vehicles. In short, inflation was wiping out the purchasing power of the dollar.

But from the mid-'80s through the 1990s, dramatically declining interest rates helped create one of the greatest Bull Markets in U.S. market history. Fueled by tech stocks and Y2K concerns, the Dow Jones Industrial Average, the S & P and the NASDAQ all posted unbelievable, annual gains – all of which allowed investors to become accustomed to doubling and tripling their monies within one to two years on tech stocks and/or "hot" Internet start-ups.

By the mid-'90s, I was approaching 25 years in the financial services field and started to see the value of determining the growth rates my clients needed to earn in order to achieve their lifetime goals, which typically amounted to anywhere from 5 to 8 percent on their investable assets. To make this happen, I counseled clients to look at, and utilize, more conservative investment vehicles and to use asset allocation to reach the growth rate needed to achieve their retirement goals.

Greed, however, was running rampant by the late-'90s and many clients were unhappy with even a 15 to 20 percent return, especially when their friends were doubling and tripling their money on high-flying equity holdings. But in March of 2000, the bubble burst and the biggest Bear Market since the Great Depression reared its ugly head. For example, the NASDAQ peaked at the 5,000 level in 2000, but in less than two years it had declined 75 percent, the largest drop of any equity index in the history of the U.S. stock market.

After watching investors lose millions of dollars during this downturn by trying to chase astronomical returns in equities, I realized how important our strategy of determining the growth rates that our clients needed to earn in order to achieve their lifetime goals had become. Even today, with market uncertainties brought about by a host of economic and political factors, my approach to investing has remained the same: I work with clients to determine the growth rate they will need and help them invest their money accordingly using asset allocation to achieve a growth rate that is calculated using a special retirement funding analysis developed by our firm (you can visit <u>www.larashullmay.com</u> for more details).

Why is it so important to determine the growth rate needed to achieve your retirement goals? The simple answer is this: Most investors take too much risk. If a couple can achieve ALL of their lifetime and retirement goals by earning just 4 percent, WHY take the risk of investing in the equity markets? Instead, why not just invest in U.S. Treasury Bonds and government-backed mortgage bonds at 4.8 percent and 5.5 percent respectively (at the time of this writing)?

Realistically, though, most people cannot achieve their retirement goals with a growth rate of less than 5 percent. Given this, I decided to write this book in order to encourage investors and other financial advisors to follow the strategies I have developed and used with great success. Bottom line, it is all about identifying a set of lifetime goals and then determining a growth rate needed on your investments to meet them. Is this possible in today's up-and-down marketplace? Yes, it is; and I believe it can be accomplished by following a careful strategy that does two things: 1) determine the growth rate needed to achieve your retirement and lifetime goals; and 2) utilize asset allocation to attain your desired growth rate.

Great things are possible when it comes to saving for retirement. However, it takes careful planning and commitment to a solid strategy that always remains focused on your lifetime goals. Are you up to the challenge? Are you ready to possibly re-think your approach to retirement? These questions and more will need to be answered by the time you have completed this book.

So as you go through the following chapters, I encourage you to not only read, but get involved with the information I am sharing with you. Grab a pencil and paper and be ready to work. And be ready to put some careful thought into what the future holds. Just reading, and not doing the exercises or applying the information to your own situation, will do you no good.

With all this in mind, I wish you the best because your Retirement Success Solution is right in front of you!

E. Ronald Lara, CFP

Chapter One

Your Reasons for Retiring

Retiring is an admirable goal for anyone, no matter their present (or expected) financial situation. The key, though, is to first determine WHY you want to retire, not HOW you are going to retire.

Why do you want to retire, either now or later? Do you have a plan for what you are going to do when you retire? If so, does this plan take into account not only your financial needs, but your physical and mental ones as well? You have probably thought about the "upsides," but have you identified the "downsides" of retiring? These questions and more need to be considered and answered before you retire. Why? Well, your well being may depend upon it.

When working with clients, one of my first – and key – questions is, "Do you want to retire?" A common response is something like, "Well, I'm 65, so I guess I better." In my mind, there is no right or wrong answer because how you approach the issue of retirement depends on many different variables.

Unfortunately, I've known individuals who decided to retire when they were 65 – either because they felt it was time, or they worked for companies that had a mandatory retirement age. In both cases, these people basically ended up sitting around and watching television all day; this is what their retirement was all about. Consequently (and not surprisingly), they weren't happy about retirement. They gained weight and got out of shape, and some even passed away in their early seventies, despite a history of long life in their family.

I have a client (whom we will call Joe) who used to work for a granite tile company. He has invested with me over the past 20 years, thus reaping the success of the rising stock market during the 1980s and 1990s. By the summer of 2000, he had a portfolio of approximately $1,000,000 - much more than he had ever dreamed of having.

Because he was 65 he had to take mandatory retirement from his company and start drawing on his union pension plan. In addition to this pension plan, he also started to receive social security benefits and had a rental property that produced $18,000 of annual income. Bottom line, he was rolling in the dough and didn't even need to tap into his main portfolio. The problem was this: While he planned on having the money to retire, he didn't plan on what to do when he retired, so he was unhappy after he retired. Because of this he has gained significant weight over the past five years and spends most of his time shuffling around the house with no real purpose.

My point is simple: Deciding to retire just because you are 60, 65, 70, or whatever age is not a good enough reason to take such a big step. In fact, I believe many people retire prematurely without taking a look at the "big picture."

There are some people who have thought long and hard about retirement and have a specific plan in mind. Maybe they want to travel, or maybe they want to do nothing all – no matter the situation, if you have the resources to do whatever you want, then by all means do what makes you happy. But I strongly believe that if you can continue to work, while avoiding the things you don't want to do, you will be much happier in the long run. How can this be? In short, by taking this approach you will be happy about getting up in the morning and doing whatever it is you want to do that day – whether it is a new job, volunteering, a hobby, traveling, participating in sports or even mentoring others.

Unfortunately, many people have simply not thought about what they really want to do post-retirement, nor have they really determined when they want to stop working. In this case, I usually recommend people continue working, even if they have the financial means to retire right away. Why? Well, I have found that continuing to work full-time, or even part-time, does wonders for your pocketbook, as well as your health. And many clients who have decided to go down this path have told me this was the best thing they have ever done.

One of my good friend's father is living proof of the benefits of this "keep working" strategy. At 99, Harvey is remarkably healthy and mentally sharp, something he attributes to the fact that he still works. In fact, he recently celebrated his 25th anniversary at a job he started when he went back to work at 72 years of age!

My father's situation was similar. He started his last job at age 59 and retired at 84 with 25 years of service. While he worked, he enjoyed a more active social life, was excited about getting up in the morning, and, more importantly, enjoyed outstanding mental and physical health. However, he kicked himself within six months of retiring because he quit working too soon. How could this be? For my father, it wasn't about money or time or career goals. It was all about the physical energy and mental strength he derived from doing something challenging, rewarding and productive every day. The year before he decided to retire he looked liked he was in his sixties. After retiring, he appeared to age 15 years, so by his 85th birthday he looked 85.

At the end of the day, retirement is about having the financial freedom to do whatever you want to do, whether it's traveling, volunteering for a worthy cause, or continuing to work. But it is also a time in your life when you really need to ask yourself, "What do I want to do?" Surprised? You shouldn't be, because with medical advances and improved healthcare, people are living longer than ever. So if you decide to retire at 65 or even 70, there is a good possibility that you could still have 10, 15 or even 20 more productive years. Given this, you need to know what you want to do and then determine whether or not you have the financial means to make it happen.

One way to accomplish this is to not go "cold turkey" when it comes time for retirement, meaning don't quit working all together. Instead, I recommend you evaluate your present work situation and then find ways to eliminate those things you don't like. Is this really possible? Of course it is, but it's an option that people readily admit they have not considered. Once again, work doesn't have to be unpleasant. The key is to focus on the quality of the work experience and the satisfaction you derive from it.

Keep in mind, continuing to work does not mean you have to keep doing what you are presently doing – sometimes that isn't possible, or even desirable. If this is the case, you need to find something in another field that may interest you. For example, I have a client who is a doctor and when it came time for him to hang up his stethoscope, he knew he wanted to keep working, but not in the medical field. He did, however, have an interest in cooking and it just so happened that his daughter was a caterer. Can you guess what he does now? You got it – at 76 years young, he now works part-time as a cook for his daughter's catering business. Needless to say, he loves his new career, mainly because it gets him out of the house and keeps him busy doing something he enjoys.

My point is this: Retiring should never mean you quit living, or even working. Retirement should be viewed as another important step in your life – one where you focus your energy and time on doing things you want to do. To make this happen, though, you need to have a plan in place and the financial resources to allow this freedom and flexibility – which is why following a sound strategy of saving and investing and utilizing asset allocation is so critical to your future success.

Tips You Can Use

If you are interested in still working instead of retiring "cold turkey," here are some things you can do to get yourself started down the right retirement road:

- Draw a line down the middle of a piece of paper. On the right side, write down all the negatives about your job (what you don't like about it). On the left side, jot down everything you like about your job. When you are done, you should have a clearer picture of what kind of job you might consider pursuing instead of retiring. (I learned this strategy from The Strategic Coach program founded by Dan Sullivan. Dan calls it The Retirement Trick®)

Things I like about my job	Things I don't like about my job

- If you are not interested in continuing the same kind of work you are doing now, make a "wish list" of the activities or types of jobs you would like to do, whether full-time, part-time or volunteer. Take this list and work with an outside agency to help you find an employer and/or organization that might have opportunities for someone like yourself. If you are looking for paid opportunities, work with an employment agency that helps place permanent or temporary workers. But if you are interested in volunteering in a particular field, many social service organizations maintain updated lists of volunteer opportunities in their particular community. Either way, there are plenty of resources out there for anyone interested in starting a new career path.

* TM & © 2005, The Strategic Coach Inc. All rights reserved. Used with permission. www.strategiccoach.com

E. Ronald Lara, CFP

Chapter Two

Making Your Future Exciting

If you have decided to retire now or determined when you might like to, there are some important things you need to do – starting right now.

No matter what your retirement timeline turns out to be, some significant planning is needed. Most importantly, you need to determine what it is you want to do. Do you want to travel? Do you want to volunteer your time? Do you want to work a part-time job? Do you want to go back to school? Whatever your course of action, you need to start laying the foundation now for the things you will be doing down the road when you have more time and resources available.

Simply put, if you do not plan now, you may find yourself waking up each morning with nothing more to look forward to than another day filled with endless hours of television, occasionally broken-up by a visit to the refrigerator during commercial breaks – all the while bemoaning the fact that you aren't good enough to join the senior golf tour. Is this really how you want to spend your retirement? I hope not, because so much more is possible if you put some things down on paper and develop a comprehensive plan.

At the age of 65, an attorney from a prestigious law firm retired, but he didn't plan it very well, and he didn't have any outside interests and/or hobbies to fall back on. So the first Monday of his retirement he asked his wife what they were going to do. She said, "Honey, I don't know what you're going to do, but I have my own plans," and simply left him home alone.

All of us have heard the quote "I married you for better or for worse, but not for lunch." Well, in this case, this man apparently didn't take those words to heart, because he sits at home, watches TV and drinks his occasional beer (unfortunately with greater frequency as time goes on). Because of this his health has deteriorated, so that now he has neither the energy nor the strength to travel, which is what his wife really loves to do.

This story is a great example of why I believe planning and setting goals is so important. And because of this belief, I want you to take the time to conduct an exercise that has changed my own life, given it direction, and added some excitement.

Set aside at least an hour to begin the work, find a place where you will not be interrupted, and set yourself up with blank paper and a pencil or two. If you are married or have a significant other, it's important to do this exercise with your partner, because he or she will likely play a big part in the process. You are about to draw up a road map for your retirement, as well as for the rest of your life.

Begin by making a list of all the things you want to do in retirement, including some of the things you would like to have accomplished by the end of your life. Write down all of them, and don't be afraid to include some farfetched, lofty goals you have always wanted to achieve, but never thought you could. Put it all out there – be sure to daydream a little and visualize yourself fulfilling some of those dreams.

Now lay out a timeline for achieving these goals. Begin by setting up a long-term timeline with intermediate steps.

An example will show you what I mean.

Goals:

1. Break 85 in Golf
2. Get part-time consulting job
3. Volunteer for a charitable organization
4. Travel to all major continents
5. Maintain cholesterol level below 175
6. Take courses with my spouse
7. Hike the Himalayas
8. Learn a new sport
9. Read a book per month
10. Take cooking lessons

Now that you have listed some goals, break each goal down into mini goals. For example, if you shoot 100 in golf, set a time frame to shoot 95, then 90, and finally your goal of 85. Your planning for getting to your goal of 85 might look like this:

Goal: Break 85 in Golf

Step 1: Sign up for golf lessons Time: Two months from now break 95

Step 2. Practice three times per week Time: Three months from now break 90

Step 3. Attend golf school

Step 4. Set up schedule with golf pro to Time: Four months from start break 85

Analyze your game

Achieving the rest of your goals is similar. Set time lines for completion of intermediate steps toward fulfillment of your goals. For example, if you want to hike the Himalayas, your steps might include 1) searching on the internet for commercial trekkers in the Himalayas. You would give yourself a timeline for collecting information. Then, 2) you would determine the cost for you and your spouse. If the cost is too high, set your timeline for taking the trip a year or two out and put the monies aside each month. If the trip costs $12,000, set aside $500 per month in a separate vacation account so the funds are available when you need them.

The key is to plan. With travel costs within the reach of most of us, economical trips are available to almost any place in the world. You can actually go to the places you've always dreamt of visiting.

Keep in mind that the goals you initially set down are not necessarily set in stone. You may wish to go back and change some of the things on your original list as circumstances dictate. Maybe your financial situation changes due to any number of reasons or maybe something happens in your life (like a death or illness) that forces you to re-evaluate both your short and long-term goals. Either way, these (or a host of other circumstances) may require you to re-asses your goals and change them accordingly.

The main thing, though, is to have some defined goals – goals that reflect what you want to do and where you want to be during your 'golden years' – and to do whatever you can in order to move in a positive fashion toward attaining them.

Given all this, our next step – finding a way to pay for it all- is just as important. So looking at the financial aspects of achieving these goals must not be taken lightly. And I can think of no better way to drive this point home than to share another story.

Bob and Nadine have been clients of mine for the past six years. When I first met them they were both successful in their own careers and they had managed to sock away a significant amount of money. In short, they had accumulated about $1,700,000 in investable assets for their retirement, along with another $7,000,000 in illiquid assets.

Both of them wanted to retire in 2000, but they had never sat down and really discussed what it was they wanted in retirement. Nor had they identified what it was they wanted to have accomplished by the end of their lives.

So after having decided to transfer their accounts to our firm, they proceeded to go through the planning exercise of making their lists of goals and formulating their timelines for retirement and lifetime achievements. By the end of their first hour of planning, Nadine and Bob were very excited about what they could realistically accomplish, and, more importantly, each had finally realized what was important to the other.

For example, they learned that they were both concerned about the wealth their children would inherit and how it would impact their lives. Likewise, Nadine learned that Bob had a yearning to sail across the Atlantic, while Bob discovered that Nadine wanted to pursue a degree in interior design.

So by the end of a second hour of planning they had begun to refine their timelines for achieving their goals and had initiated the process of defining steps for reaching them. We started by establishing a private foundation for them which their children now manage. In fact, their kids are now more interested in the foundation getting the bulk of their parents' inheritance and in doing something worthwhile with those funds than in inheriting the money for themselves. Simply put, this has given Bob and Nadine peace of mind that bears no price tag.

Since that first meeting, Nadine has also earned her degree in interior design and now works part-time for an interior design business. And in May of 2005, Bob set sail across the Atlantic, traveling from Spain to the Virgin Islands on a 51-foot sloop.

By making the commitment to plan, to create goal lists, to set up time lines, to define and analyze their own desires and dreams, they now have a clear picture of what goals they want to achieve and a timeline and plan for achieving them. We were also able to invest their assets to minimize their federal and state income taxes, and to allocate assets to attain the growth rate needed to reach their lifetime goals.

This is what the process is all about, and it offers an excellent example of how it can work for you if you are willing to commit to the effort required.

Tips You Can Use

Preparing for retirement and experiencing the excitement of your dreams into your life depends, in part, on your ability to identify what it is you want to do and to accomplish. Having said this, here are a couple of things you can start doing today.

- When people set goals, they tend to under-sell themselves. Given this, don't be afraid to THINK BIG and write down goals that may seem tough to attain, even over a long time horizon.

- After writing down your goals put them in a picture frame and place them in plain sight where you can see them every day, so that they serve as a constant reminder of what you need to accomplish.

E. Ronald Lara, CFP

Chapter Three

Determining How Much You Really Need

Now that you've determined what your goals are for the next few years, it's time to figure out how much money you're going to need to make all of this possible. Are you up to the task? I hope so, because this is an important step in any financial planning process.

I believe most people already have a good idea of how much money they spend per month and what kind of income they need to maintain their chosen standard of living. In the case of my clients, the average person has about $1,000,000 set aside for retirement, but is also looking for $7,000 per month in available income. With these amounts, does the math work? That depends on a number of factors (i.e. expenditures) leading up to their actual time of retirement. What about you? What annual income do you require? If you don't know, now is the time to take a look at what you will need and begin the planning process.

A good first step to determine how much money you will need to achieve all your lifetime goals is to look at your annual take home income and savings rate. For example, if your present take-home income is $83,000 and you're able to save $11,000 of that amount, your annual income requirement is $72,000 – the amount you will need to plan for (and save) as retirement nears.

However, you need to be generous in your estimate of income needs because it's better to have more income than you need at retirement than to come up short. There are also several financial-related matters you need to take into consideration when determining your future needs – all of which can either increase your income requirement or decrease your investable assets.

For example, here are some things that can INCREASE the amount of money you will eventually need for retirement:

- Education costs for children and/or grandchildren
- Care needs for aging parents
- Long-term care premiums
- Life insurance premiums for estate planning
- Increased health insurance premiums (if retiring before Medicare kicks-in)
- Wedding expenditures (this can be big if you have several daughters!)
- Luxury purchases (i.e. second homes, lakeside cabins, boats, RVs, etc.)
- Planned travel (i.e. yearly cruises, trips overseas, etc.)
- However, there are also some factors that can REDUCE your future income needs:

- Paying off your home mortgage
- Refinancing your mortgage
- Eligibility for Medicare
- Absence of work related expenses (i.e. clothing, commuting costs, lunches, etc.)
- Working part-time

What does all this mean? Hopefully, it demonstrates that you simply can't pull a number out of thin air and think it will be right. Determining how much money you will need requires some careful thought and planning. This is why it's helpful to use some type of template to not only assess your overall financial situation, but also to compute the amount of growth needed in order to achieve your retirement goals.

Let's say you have accumulated approximately $1 million in assets which constitutes your "nest egg" (i.e. the amount you intend to use for your retirement). However, you need to insure that major expenses are taken into account and subtracted from the overall figure. In short, this will give you the amount of assets you will be able to invest in order to produce the retirement income you will need for the rest of your life.

Below is an example of how major expenses need to be viewed. Notice how each event/expense, current estimated costs, number of years until completion, and inflation are all used to determine the amount you need today to pay for it in the future. I've done the math for you.

How Major Expenses Can Impact Your Retirement Portfolio:

Future Lump Sum Expenses in Retirement

Item		Cost	# of payments	Inflation Rate	Years till Expense	Present Value of expense
Wedding for daughter		$40,000	1	5.00%	4	$43,198
Vacation Home Deposit		$30,000	1	5.00%	1	$30,583
New Boat		$25,000	1	5.00%	1	$25,980
New Sports Car		$60,000	4	3.00%	0	$55,756
Grandson's College		$18,000	4	5.00%	3	$57,893
Discount Rate =	3.00%					$213,411

Assuming the person in the above example has $1 million in investable assets they would need to subtract *$213,411* from this amount – which would mean they have *$785,589* in assets available for retirement. For your own purposes, you can go to our website (www.larashullmay.com) and use our on-line templates, which will do the above calculations for you.

The tallying, however, doesn't end here because the next step is taking this adjusted "assets available for retirement" figure and adding it to your other sources of income.

For example, here's a list of retirement income sources potentially available to you:

- Social Security
- Pension income
- Rental income
- Alimony payments and/or child support
- Deferred compensation
- Trust income
- Annuity income
- Charitable trust income

Now that you've determined how much spendable income is needed for retirement, you need to determine the gross amount of income you must plan for after the payment of federal and state income taxes. You will also need to determine exactly how much you must withdraw from your qualified retirement plans (like IRAs) to minimize the impact of federal and state income taxes – assuming, of course, that most of you have rolled over your 401(k) and/or 403(B) plans into an IRA, along with any lump sum payments from your pension or profit sharing plans.

Trust me, it isn't as difficult (or complicated) as it may sound, but it's certainly one of many important steps you need to take – and it's all a part of the Retirement Success Solution! I'll show you how to do this in the next chapter.

Tips You Can Use:

Financial planning for the future can be a big task, but it's an important one. Given this, consider the following when determining how you might better use (or allocate) your money:

- When considering major, lump sum expenses, be sure not to short-change yourself. It's better to plan for something that "might happen," as compared to not planning for it at all. For example, you dream of owning a motorhome but don't know if you will have the money. It's better to plan on this expense (or a portion of it) now, as opposed to not figuring on it at all. That's why it's so important to list it in the table above and subtract that cost from the retirement assets that will be used solely to provide retirement income. If you don't allow for major expenses in the beginning of your retirement, when you are first starting to withdraw monies from your retirement assets, you will be very reluctant to withdraw those assets, for that major purchase, from those assets that are generating income.

- If you feel your list of anticipated lump sum expenses is getting too long or pricey based on your expected retirement income, consider cutting back on things and/or downsizing your expectations. For example, do you need both a boat and lake home? Or is there a way you can plan now for a smaller boat and/or consider purchasing a vacation home in a location where real estate prices aren't as high?

- Bottom line, don't be afraid to fine-tune your "wish list" and estimated expenses. Why? Because making your retirement planning (and saving) strategy work, you have to be behind it 100 percent.

Chapter Four

Income Sources, Tax Savings and Withdrawal Strategies

Now that you've determined how much you need for retirement, the next critical step is to find a way to make it all happen. This can seem to be a daunting task, but it doesn't need to be because so much is possible (and attainable) if you follow a carefully structured plan of attack when it comes to your retirement planning.

Nonetheless, after looking at the figure you came up with in the previous chapter, you still might be thinking (no matter what I say), "How in the world am I going to make this work?" First of all, don't worry – at least not now. Yes, all those lump sum expenses (and "big purchases") can start adding up very quickly, but just because the numbers seem intimidating doesn't mean you should shy away from trying to attain your retirement goals.

The key is this: You should be excited about your future! And I want you to realize that thinking this way, and putting that enthusiasm into your savings and planning strategies, can help make all those expenses and obligations seem insignificant in the long run. Once again, what it takes is careful, strategic planning no matter how much money you have now, or plan to have in the future.

Having said all this, how and where you get your retirement income after retirement is important. Here's an example of why you need to think carefully about this:

A client of mine, who was a sheet metal worker, retired when he was only 60 percent vested in his company's retirement plan. He wasn't forced to retire due to health or age reasons, and he could have worked longer, but he just thought it was time to be done – he'd had it in his mind that he wanted to retire at a certain age and didn't want to budge from that. I'm all for people making a plan and sticking to it, but in this case he could have made his retirement much more comfortable if he had waited a bit longer. How so? By waiting just two more years before retiring, he would have been 100 percent vested at retirement and enjoyed $1,400 more per month for the rest of his life!

Just think what you could do with an extra $1,400 per month! Think of how many more trips you could take while retired, or consider how that money could be applied to any number of "dream purchases." Bottom line, money like that can add up to a significant amount over one's lifetime. Moreover, this story demonstrates how overlooking key details can cost you dearly in the long run.

What's your present situation like? Are you totally vested in a company pension plan or are you ready to quit early? If not fully vested, are you taking part in other retirement savings offerings available to you? It's important to answer these questions and take a close look – just like you did with anticipated expenses – at what income sources you will have in the future.

Here are some income sources many people rely upon during retirement, some of which were already mentioned in the previous chapter. I've provided comments on some of them for you. They are:

- Social Security
- Pension plans
- Rental income
- Trust income (Note: Usually set up by a parent or grandparent)
- Deferred compensation (Note: Identify for how many years and if there are any conditions attached to receiving the income)
- Life insurance policies (Note: Do you really need the coverage if you provide no economic benefit to your family? Consider cashing-in the policy or, better yet, see an agent who can get you a viatecal settlement. This is a process where you sell your policy to an organization that will give you more than the cash surrender value for your policy)
- Annuity income

- If the above sources are possible income streams, let's now list asset sources that can be used to generate income in retirement:

- 401(k) plans

- Individual Retirement Accounts (IRAs)
- 403(b) plans (Note: Normally offered through non-profit organizations)
- 457 plans (Note: Deferred compensation plans offered through non-profit organizations)
- Money market and saving accounts
- Individual stocks and bonds
- Certificates of Deposit (CDs)
- Deferred compensation plans
- Stock option plans
- Investment real estate
- Mutual funds
- Home equity

Granted, some of these options – like deferred compensation plans and stock options – are not available to everyone. But they are examples of asset sources that people sometimes fail to take into account when planning for their future.

The key is to make sure you've made an accurate assessment of your ENTIRE portfolio before leaping into retirement. To do this, I recommend you prepare a detailed financial statement and update it at the end of each year and make sure assets to be used for retirement are clearly identified. Given all this, you can see I believe there's much more to retirement than sitting back and waiting for your social security and pension checks to come in!

As I've already pointed out, effectively managing your retirement assets takes planning. In order to achieve all the goals you outlined in Chapter 2, you need to make sure you're maximizing the full potential of your assets. And the only way to do this is to take a long-term, strategic approach to tap into your retirement sources.

Two of the most important things to consider are how much to withdraw from your qualified assets and how much to withdraw from your non-qualified assets in order to minimize your federal and state income taxes. Below is an example of what I mean.

For the purposes of this exercise, assume that the couple is filing jointly and currently receiving the following income:

- Social Security Income = $20,000
- Pension & Rental Income = $21,000

Now let us look at the following tax tables for a couple filing jointly in the year 2005:

Tax Rate Schedule – Married Filing Jointly

Tax Rate	From	To
10%	$0.00	$14,600
15%	$14,601	$59,400
25%	$59,401	$119,950
28%	$119,951	$182,800
33%	$182,801	$326,450
35%	$326,451	And above

For example, if you have $20,000 coming to you from social security and have another $21,000 coming from a company pension plan and rental income, how much should you be withdrawing from qualified plan assets such as 401(k)s or IRAs, and how much should you be withdrawing from your personal investments? The answer will result in considerably lower federal and state income taxes than simply withdrawing from your qualified retirement assets.

Ideally, you would want to keep your taxable income at $59,400 (or lower) because the tax on $59,400 is only 15 percent. However, every dollar of taxable income above $59,400 is taxed at 25 percent (or higher if your taxable income is considerable).

I have included a table below that explains my point, as well as a template for you to use to compute the ideal withdrawal rates from your retirement account (IRA) and non-qualified (personal) investments.

Let's assume our retired couple, who have approximately $1,000,000 in IRA assets and an additional $500,000 in personal investments, would like to have $100,000 in spendable income per year during retirement. They also receive $20,000 from social security (of which 85 percent is taxable, or $17,000), $11,000 in rental income and $10,000 from a small pension plan. Given this, how much should they withdraw from their IRA, and how much should they withdraw from their personal investments?

Look at the table below:

$59,400	Beginning of 25% tax bracket
$ 6,200	Add 2 personal exemptions @ $3,100 each
$12,000	Add mortgage interest
$ 4,000	Add real estate taxes
$ 6,500	Add property taxes
$ 1,150	Add charitable giving
$ 2,750	Add state inc taxes @ 4.63% of $59,400 CO res.
$92,000	Gross income with Federal income tax of $8,180

The $92,000 represents how much taxable income our retired couple can have and remain in the 15% tax bracket with the above itemized deductions.

As you can see, I've listed their current itemized deductions and entered them in the table above. (Note: If you have taxable income of $92,000, along with the itemized deductions above, your taxable income after deductions will be $59,400, which is ideal because this is the point where you go from the 15 percent tax bracket up to the 25 percent tax bracket).

Now let's subtract, from the $92,000 of income above, the amount of taxable income we will be receiving. The first source of taxable income is social security and it's important to remember that 85 percent of this is taxable. Once again, other sources of taxable income during retirement may include:

- Pension income
- Rental income
- Trust income
- Deferred compensation
- Annuity income
- Part-time income, consulting and/or other 1099 income

Now let's see what *taxable* income they have:

$17,000	Taxable SS benefits – 85% ($20,000) are taxable
$10,000	Taxable Pension Benefits
$11,000	Taxable Rental Income
$38,000	**Total Taxable Income**

See how the example above shows taxable income of $38,000? Subtracting this figure from the $92,000 of adjustable gross income leaves $54,000, which is the ideal amount to withdraw from your IRA. So any other income needed should be withdrawn from your personal investments, where it will not be taxed as ordinary income. However, if you withdraw more than $54,000 from your IRA you will be taxed at 25 percent of the excess, plus the percentage that corresponds with whatever state tax bracket you might fall under at the time. (And it's important to point out that you should limit the withdrawals from your IRA to 6 percent annually. Why is this? See Chapter 7 of this book for a detailed response to this often asked question.)

In the above scenario, the adjusted gross income for our couple would be:

$54,000	IRA Withdrawal
$17,000	Social Security Income
$10,000	Pension Income
$11,000	Rental Income
$92,000	Adjusted Gross Income

Subtracting their itemized deductions, plus $6,200 for personal exemptions, results in:

$92,000	Adjusted Gross Income
- $32,600	Itemized Deductions + Personal Exemptions
$59,400	Taxable Income

The resulting federal income tax would be $8,180, plus their state income tax (I'll use Colorado here) of $2,750 for a total of:

$8,180	Federal Income Tax
$2,750	State Income Tax
$10,930	Total Federal & State Income tax

Thus, for our couple who wanted $100,000 of spendable income they will need to have total income of:

$100,000	Spendable Income
$ 10,930	Federal & State Income Taxes
$110,930	Total Income required

*(If you are using our Retirement Funding Analysis software on our web site this is the **gross** amount that you should enter under "Annual Income Desired". Obviously, you will use your own figures but you should enter the gross amount that includes the federal and state income taxes you will pay plus the amount of spendable income you desire.)*

Our couple's sources of income would be as follows:

$ 20,000	Social Security Income
$ 10,000	Pension Income
$ 11,000	Rental Income
$ 54,000	Ideal IRA withdrawal
$ 15,930	Withdrawal from Personal Investments
$110,930	Total Income
$ 10,930	Less Federal & State Income Taxes
$100,000	Net Spendable Income

Does this all make sense? If not, don't worry, because seeking out the assistance of an experienced financial planner will help clarify these steps and strategies. Nonetheless, these questions and more need to be carefully considered and become an integral part of your overall planning process, which is why it's important to fully understand what income sources you have at your disposal.

So for now, I encourage you to make a "master list" of all your income sources and identify what value (dollar wise) each of them has right now, as well as what you anticipate they will be worth in the future– ballpark figures will do for now. It's more important that you take the time to identify these future income sources and become very familiar with what they are, how they work, and any rules they have in regard to distributions.

Tips You Can Use:

Keeping track of, and safeguarding, your retirement assets is important. Here are some things you can do to make sure you are properly managing your money:

- Anyone who owns IRAs, mutual funds, individual stocks, and other investments knows how many forms and statements they can generate. However, these documents are important, so keeping them all in one place – where they can be easily accessed and reviewed – is important. Make sure you keep a complete list of your investments – with company names, account numbers and contact information – in a separate, safe location (i.e., a safety deposit box, an office, a relative, etc.). If your home is damaged by fire or flood or any other calamity, having this information safely tucked away will save you a lot of headaches, especially if you don't have any statements or documents indicating your current account balances.

- I also recommend you compile a list of all your assets and tell someone where it is kept. Also include the location of important papers (like your will, deeds on real estate or owned insurance policies) and give this list to a relative or friend you can trust to hold it in the event of an emergency.

- Don't get sucked into the time consuming trap of checking on your accounts all the time. I know it's tempting to check the stock tables in the paper or watch the pundits on television, but you have better things to do in retirement than worry about what the market is doing every second of the day. Be familiar with your accounts and pay attention to what's going on in the news, but fine-tuning or adjusting your portfolio isn't needed every day – every other week or even monthly is much more realistic.

- Adding some "extra income" to your portfolio can make a big difference in the things you can afford to do during retirement. Having said this, work with a financial planner to see if working a part-time job might be a good fit for you. Keep in mind, working part-time not only provides more income but also gives you something positive and worthwhile to focus on, as opposed to sitting around your home wondering what you're going to do next.

- While actively setting aside and saving money for retirement is important, maintaining this habit after you retire is also beneficial. Think about it - no one knows for sure how long they're going to live, so a long-range approach to savings is always recommended. So whether you're planning for retirement or already enjoying it, setting aside money each month in interest and/or dividend income generating accounts is a "good habit" to develop.

Chapter Five

Tax Strategies and Tax Law Changes Worth Noting

Like the old adage goes: There are two certainties in life – death and taxes. We won't talk about death here, but taxes are certainly something we need to discuss because they can have a tremendous impact on your retirement portfolio if you don't plan properly.

In short, you need to take the necessary steps to integrate your retirement planning and tax planning in order to make sure your tax liabilities are fully minimized. For example, what investment vehicles are you using right now to save for retirement? Are these offering you a tax advantage? If so, great, but what kind of tax obligations will they create once you retire and start withdrawing money?

These are the types of questions you must ask yourself as you start laying the groundwork for retirement. This includes determining where you will be getting your money from once the retirement journey begins.

For example, I once worked with a couple that was already retired, but determined they were paying way too much money toward tax obligations each year. Money wasn't much of an issue for them, but they did need quite a bit of monthly income due to the lifestyle they wanted to live. Given this, finding ways to cut their tax liabilities would be helpful over the long-term. So with some minor adjustments I was able to show them how they could reduce their taxes dramatically – from $80,000 to around $11,000!

How could this happen? Well, it was just a matter of showing them how they were taking their money out of the wrong accounts. They were withdrawing money from retirement accounts which are taxed at a higher rate. So I had them start taking money out of well-funded personal accounts, which allowed them to maintain their lifestyle while significantly reducing their taxes.

I can't tell you how many times I've seen people caught in tax-related situations like the one above, where too much money is being paid toward taxes. Keep in mind that taxes cannot be avoided totally, no matter what some experts may tell you. There are, however, steps you can take to minimize the taxes you pay over the long term, even in retirement.

There are legitimate (and legal) tax strategies for everyone, no matter your situation or income. And just like the process of saving money for retirement, there's always a way to get the results you're looking for – you just have to have the creativity and will power to do it. This is why it's important to work with a proactive financial planner and/or an accountant who can advise you on steps that can be taken to reduce your taxes.

For what it's worth, here are eleven tax strategies you might want to consider:

1. Now that the capital gains tax has been reduced to 15 percent, I don't recommend purchasing a variable annuity outside of a qualified plan. Why? Because if you withdraw monies from a variable annuity the gain on the annuity is taxed as ordinary income. On the other hand, if you purchase a tax managed mutual fund the gain of the withdrawal will be taxed at a lower rate (capital gains tax rate) than a variable annuity.

The table on the next page shows the difference in tax after 10 years, assuming a 6 percent growth rate. The tax on the variable annuity is 276% percent more than the tax on the managed mutual fund.

Taxation of Variable Annuity vs. Tax Managed Mutual Fund

Variable Annuity		Tax Managed Mutual Fund	
Assumptions:		**Assumptions:**	
Federal Tax Bracket	31.00%	Capital Gains Tax Rate	15.00%
State Tax Bracket	6.00%	State Capital Gains Tax	6.00%
Effective Tax Bracket	35.14%	Combined Tax Rate	21.00%
Annual Growth Rate	6.00%	Annual Growth Rate	6.00%
Initial Investment	$100,000	Initial Investment	$ 100,000
10 Years Later	$179,085	10 Years Later	$ 179,085
Withdrawal	$!0,000	Withdrawal	$ 10,000
Federal & State Income Tax	$ 3,514	Federal & State Income Tax	$ 927
		Percentage Increase	**278.92%**

2. Purchase discounted closed-end, tax exempt bond funds that can earn you yields well in excess of 6 percent tax free. Imagine a 5 percent coupon, 15-year bond selling at par ($1,000) – its yield to maturity would be 5 percent. However, if you could buy the bond at $850 per bond, the yield to maturity on the bond would be 6.59 percent. Closed-end funds don't always sell at net asset value; they often sell at a significant discount. You can obtain the net asset value of some closed-end bond funds from your broker, so put in an order to purchase at a 12 – 15 percent discount. If you're patient, you will be rewarded with a significantly higher return than is currently available.

3. If you did purchase a variable annuity at the peak of the Bear Market and it's now in a loss position, consider cashing-in the variable annuity and taking an ordinary income tax loss on the entire amount of the loss.

4. If you have a sizeable tax loss, carry it forward (remember, though, you can only write off $3,000 of losses each year) and use an option manager to generate income by writing covered calls on blue chip stocks or the indices. The option premium will normally be in excess of 8 percent and will be considered a short-term gain. You can use this income to offset your losses and not pay tax on the option income until it exceeds your losses.

5. Transfer $5,000 of your personal assets to a Health Savings Plan each year IF your health insurance

deductible is over $1,000. The $5,000 is 100 percent tax deductible, will grow tax free, and the assets will come out tax free as long as they are used to pay for medical expenses. Trust me, as you get older you will have medical expenses!

6. If you're considering going back to school in your retirement, set up a section 529 plan for you and your spouse. While contributions aren't usually tax deductible (you may want to check with your state), they will grow tax free and come out tax free. This is also a great way to set aside educational funding gifts for grandchildren.

7. If you're selling an appreciated real estate property that has been depreciated, consider transferring the asset to a Charitable Remainder Unitrust rather than selling the property. You will avoid the recapture (which is taxed at 25 percent) and the capital gain tax, and receive a tax deduction that's based on your age and the percentage withdrawal you will be taking. Consult your tax advisor and attorney regarding these trusts.

8. If you don't need that Whole Life, Universal, or Variable Life insurance policy, consider getting a bid from a Viatecal Settlement Company before cashing it in. They could offer you considerably more for your life insurance policy than your present insurance carrier.

9. If you're thinking of buying an annuity from an insurance company, consider purchasing the annuity from a charitable institution such as your alma mater.

You will realize a substantial tax deduction that you would otherwise not receive from the insurance company.

10. Change your IRA to a SEP IRA. This will allow you to deduct 25 percent of any 1099 income you earn. If you haven't already retired, set aside as much as possible because SEP limits are 25 percent of net income, up to a maximum of $42,000 annually. This amount, however, will increase over time.

11. If you are self-employed, have no employees, and have 1099 income in excess of $200,000, consider setting up a defined benefit plan. If you're over 50, you will be able to shelter over $100,000 (or 50 percent of your income) by doing this. In short, it offers a great way to build a sizeable pension in a few years.

Bottom line, the best tax strategy for anyone is fully funding a qualified plan, like a 401(k) or an IRA. Given this, you need to max out your contributions to these types of plans because they offer the best defense, both short term and long term, against taxes. Off-the-wall, risky strategies don't need to be used, nor do you need to stop putting money into non-qualified assets, like savings accounts, money markets, and/or stocks. The key is to make sure you're putting all the money you can into your qualified plan(s).

In fact, putting the maximum amount of money into your qualified plans is such a top priority it might even be worth taking out a home equity loan in order to maximize your contributions. How so? Well, the returns on your investment that you will likely receive from a good retirement plan will probably outweigh the cost of any interest (which, by the way, is also tax deductible) you would pay on the equity loan. Never thought of it that way? Don't worry, because many people don't, unless it's explained to them. But trust me when I say it's just one good example of how being creative and proactive – not reactive – can pay-off for you in the end.

Look at the table below which shows the advantage of using a home equity loan to fund a SEP IRA.

Yes, you have an additional $100,000 mortgage but you also have $100,000 more in your SEP IRA and you have netted $17,400 from federal and state income tax savings ($35,400 less the $18,000 you spent in interest for the past five years).

It's important that you not overlook how taxes impact other aspects of your retirement portfolio. For example, when selling individual stocks and/or shares of mutual funds, how will this impact your tax liability? Should you cash out now and absorb the taxes prior to retiring, or is there a way you can hold on to these assets and use them at a later date? These are the types of questions, with the help of your planner or accountant, you need to answer now.

Advantages of Borrowing to Fund Your Retirement Plan

End of Year	Loan	Loan Rate 6%	Tax Savings @ 30%	Tax Deductible Contribution	Annual Tax Savings @ 30%
1	$20,000	$1.200	$360	$20,000	$6,000
2	$20,000	$2,300	$720	$20,000	$6,000
3	$20,000	$3,600	$1,080	$20,000	$6,000
4	$20,000	$4,800	$1,440	$20,000	$6,000
5	$20,000	$6,000	$1,800	$20,000	$6,000
TOTALS		$18,000	$5,400		$30,000

Along the same lines, you need to determine what role social security will play in your retirement plans. Keep in mind, 85 percent of your social security benefits are taxable, so figuring out how you might dampen this tax liability and/or compensate for this obligation using other income sources is important, especially if social security payments make-up a good chunk of your retirement income each month.

In the end, it's all about finding the right formula – one that factors in all your income sources, puts you in a tax bracket that works best for you, and keeps all of your lifetime goals in mind.

I've already touched on it briefly, but one of the best tax strategies in tax and retirement planning is the use of Charitable Trusts. While I could write an entire book on this subject, an example would best illustrate their benefits.

In a Charitable Trust, appreciated assets are transferred into the trust and then sold. Because the assets are in a charitable trust there's no capital gain on the sale of the assets. The taxes that would have been owed on the sale of the asset are saved.

When the Charitable Trust is set up, the grantor(s) set what percentage income they want from the trust, which usually ranges from 5 – 10 percent. There are limits on the amount that can be withdrawn, but suffice to say the older you are the more you can withdraw. Keep in mind, though, the withdrawal rate is fixed and cannot be changed once the Trust is finalized.

In addition to avoiding the capital gain tax, the grantor receives an income tax deduction on the present value of the remaining interest. I know that may sound like Greek to you, but it's determined by actuarial equations provided by the

IRS – hence the confusing nature of the concept! Because of this, the grantor actually receives two tax benefits: the first is avoiding the capital gain and the second is the income tax deduction he/she receives for the donation of the assets to the Charitable Trust.

Given all this, the withdrawal rate is paid as long as the grantor is living. And upon his death, the assets are transferred to a charity (or charities) of the donor's choosing.

To better illustrate this, let's look at the table below to see what the total tax benefits to a grantor would be by transferring $500,000 of appreciated assets with a cost basis of $250,000 to a Charitable Trust. (Note: We will assume this is a 65 year old couple who have elected an 8 percent annual withdrawal, paid quarterly).

Advantages of a Charitable Remainder Unitrust

Assumptions:

Federal Capital Gain Tax Rate	15.0%
State Capital Gain Tax Rate	6.0%
Total Capital Gain Tax Rate	21.0%
Federal Income Tax Rate	31.0%
State Income Tax Rate	6.0%
Combined Income Tax Rate	35.14%

	No Trust	C.R.U.T. Trust
Sale Price	$500,000	$500,000
Cost Basis	$250,000	$250,000
Taxable Gain on Sale	$250,000	$0.00
Capital Gain Tax on Sale	$52,500	$0.00
Tax Deduction	$0.00	$98,435*
Income Tax Savings	$0.00	$34,590
Net to Invest	$447,500	$534,590
Difference		$87,090

* Assumptions:
    Fed Mid-Term rate 5.00%
    Lifetime Payout
    8.00% Annual Payout – Paid Quarterly
    Male Age 65, Female Age 65

* NOTE: You receive a deduction of your state tax from your federal adjusted gross income thus the tax benefit is not the sum of the fed and state tax brackets.

As you can see, the couple has saved $87,090 in federal and state income taxes. At 6 percent, that's an additional $5,217 of annual income, which pays for a nice vacation each year. In addition, if the couple's estate is sizeable, transferring the assets to the Charitable Trust removes the assets from their estate, thus offering considerable estate tax savings.

Along the same line, many individuals purchase annuities from insurance companies to provide a monthly income – income they cannot outlive without the risk of investments. In an immediate annuity, annuitants receive a monthly check for as long as they live. If they live a long time, they win; if they die three months after the annuity commences, the insurance company's obligation ceases and it keeps all the money.

A better solution is to consider a gift annuity. In a gift annuity, the annuitant purchases the annuity from a charity, receives a tax deduction for the present value of the remaining interest (there's that Greek talk again), and receives the monthly check from the charity. Upon the annuitant's death, the charity, as opposed to the insurance company, retains the money.

Below is an example of what a tax deduction would be for a 65-year-old male who does a $100,000 investment in a gift annuity with a 6 percent payout:

Summary of Gift Annuity Benefits

ASSUMPTIONS

Beneficiary Age/Birth Date	65
Principal Donated	$100,000
Gift Date	3/28/2005
Payout Rate	6%
Payment Schedule	Quarterly End

BENEFITS

Charitable Deduction	$33,379
Annuity	$6,000
Tax-Free Portion	$3,348
Ordinary Income	$2,652

IRS Discount Rate is 4.6%

Given this scenario, the entire annuity becomes ordinary income after 19.9 years; and if you're contributing appreciated property the tax free portion will be reduced by the amount of capital gains reportable each year. If you're contributing short-term gain, or other ordinary income property, your deduction may be reduced. In addition, partial payments for the year of the gift will depend on the timing of your gift. However, you can enhance your deduction and increase your payout by deferring your annuity.

Granted, this may seem complicated, but there are plenty of resources out there to help you. For example, you can visit our website (www.larashullmay.com) and click on the Charitable Gift Calculator (which is on the left hand side under the Online Tools button) to do all the above calculations, as well as other charitable giving strategies which are beyond the scope of this book.

Tips You Can Use

There's more to reducing your tax liabilities than figuring out how much you need to take from Social Security and/or qualified plans each month. In fact, ownership of other valuable assets – like real estate and collectibles – can pose some problems during retirement if not handled correctly. Given this, here are some ideas you might consider to increase your income, yet not increase your taxes:

- Selling real estate can trigger a big tax payment. Instead of selling real estate holdings, create a charitable trust or consider donating the land.

- Consider doing a 1031 exchange if you are selling depreciated real estate. The recapture on depreciated real estate is 25% and a 1031 exchange allows you to defer the tax and invest the proceeds from your sale in a similar real estate property. There are a few real estate companies that have an exchange Real Estate Investment Trust (REIT) that is specifically set up for real estate exchanges. They have a diversified real estate portfolio and usually pay a 6% annual dividend.

- Where you live can have a significant impact on your taxes. For example, states like Florida, Texas, Alaska, Nevada, New Hampshire, Tennessee, Washington, Wyoming and South Dakota have no state income tax. Given this, retiring to one of these states can help your bottom line over time.

Chapter Six

The Retirement Success Solution®

So far we've gone over a number of key things that, hopefully, have you thinking about where you're headed in terms of your own retirement planning.

Clearly, planning for retirement isn't as simple as picking a random number which signifies the amount of money you THINK you will need in order to live comfortably. If it was that easy, you wouldn't be reading this book, nor would I have any need to write it – let alone be a financial planner!

As I've tried to point out, the retirement planning process requires a great deal of thought on your part, especially when it comes to identifying, and financially planning for, all those things you wish to accomplish during your lifetime. Given this, my partners and I have developed a comprehensive program which helps both individuals and couples do the following: set their retirement and lifestyle goals; develop tax and financial strategies to fit those goals; plan for legacy and health concerns; and provide knowledgeable guidance so they can feel confident about the future. This is what the Retirement Success Solution™ is all about.

The Process Defined

In its simplest form, the Retirement Success Solution® is a comprehensive, twelve-step process that is divided into three distinct stages. These stages are as follows:

Stage One

Your current situation is assessed and you receive help with setting both personal and financial goals – goals which take into account all of the things you want to do, see and/or purchase prior to, and during, your retirement years. We complete the Lifetime Focuser™ which clearly identifies your lifetime goals. The Retirement Funding Analysis is completed which determines the growth rate needed to achieve your retirement goals.

Stage Two

Working together, we develop a series of proactive investment strategies, as well as a Retirement Success Plan™ to achieve your lifetime goals. In short, these efforts will address your short- and long-term goals and provide you a proven "roadmap" to follow along the way.

Stage Three

We work together to create a Retirement Success Team™ and take the necessary steps to implement the overall plan we've developed. Remember, the end product at this point is a plan designed specifically for you, so now is the time to move forward!

The End Result

What you gain from completing the Retirement Success Solution® process will depend on your honest participation and commitment, as well as your enthusiasm for following our recommendations.

Most of the people I've worked with on this process tell me they feel more comfortable making the transition from employment to retirement after doing so. They also enjoy the feeling of greater optimism that comes from knowing that someone is guiding them along the way. Again, this is why having a knowledgeable planner in your corner to assist you is so vitally important.

People also tell me they like the fact that they have more effective tax and investment strategies in place once they're done. And they like how the process helps them develop a set of clearly defined and achievable goals. They also feel more comfortable knowing their accountant has worked with their financial planner to find the best tax strategies available.

Why is all of this important? To me it's quite simple: I believe too many people are taking too much risk when it comes to saving for retirement. This is, in part, because they have unrealistic expectations when it comes to returns, thus causing them to use investment vehicles that are more prone to wide fluctuations and losses. To combat this, the Retirement Success Solution™, using the information you provide, will help to determine the growth rate you need to achieve your retirement goals and to develop the strategies for achieving those goals.

Just do it!

Now that you know what it's all about, it's time to work your way through our Retirement Funding Analysis and see what the process can do for you. You can accomplish this by visiting our firm's website at <u>www.larashullmay.com</u> and follow the steps outlined on the site. It's really that simple. Good luck!

Tips You Can Use

Information you need to have

Before you start the Retirement Funding Analysis, you will need to have some information available in order to complete the process. So take time now to gather – or consider – your answers in the following areas:

1. Age you plan on retiring
2. Gross amount of income you want to retire on – we did this exercise in chapter 4
3. Retirement assets at death – this must exceed by at least $1.00 the total of your current retirement assets and personal assets.
4. Inflation rate
5. To what age retirement income must last (plan on living longer than you think you will)
6. Total retirement assets available
7. Annual retirement contributions (both employee and employer)
8. Personal investment assets that will be used for retirement
9. Personal annual savings until retirement
10. Deferred compensation lump sum payments
11. Deferred compensation annual benefits (and for how long you will receive them)
12. Stock option details
13. Pension income
14. Social Security benefits for you and your spouse
15. Rental income
16. Other sources of income

17. Potential inheritances and conservative estimate of when you will receive them
18. Cost of living increases on Social Security benefits
19. Cost of living increases on pension income if applicable

Doing It On Your Own

If you decide to do your own retirement planning (which I don't recommend), here are some steps that you should follow in order to get the most out of your efforts:

1. Identify your after tax income needs (as we discussed earlier) then determine the gross dollars before taxes needed for retirement.
2. Identify the lump sum expenses you will have in retirement and subtract these costs from the available assets you have for retirement.
3. Complete our Retirement Funding Analysis at our website (www.larashullmay.com) to determine the growth rate you need to earn on your retirement and personal assets in order to achieve your retirement goals.
4. If the growth rate needed is in excess of 7 percent, work with a professional financial planner to develop tax and investment strategies that will reduce this rate below 7 percent because the probability of achieving a return at this level over a 20-year period is only slightly above 50 percent.
5. Asset allocate your assets to achieve your targeted growth rate.

6. Select top decile managers in each asset class so you have the peace of mind of knowing you only have the best managers working for you.
7. IF you can achieve all of your retirement and lifetime goals by just investing in U.S. Treasury Bonds, do it. Otherwise, why take the risk?
8. Rebalance your portfolio at least annually.
9. Set up a goal sheet chart which shows where you should be at the end of each quarter and track your performance so you can measure your progress against your goals.
10. Re-define your goals each year and make sure you're asset allocated to achieve your desired growth rate.

Now that you have determined the growth rate needed to achieve your retirement goals, you need to track your progress to make sure you are achieving your goals.

I use our Retirement Success Solution Goal Sheet™ to track our clients' assets and show them where they are in the process. Whether you are in the accumulating assets stage or you have retired and are withdrawing assets from your retirement accounts, the goal sheet gives you a visual picture of your progress.

An example of our goal sheet is the best way to show what I mean.

Meet Joe Simpson, born 12/15/1943, age 62, who wishes to retire in three years with an annual income of $120,000. Joe and his wife have accumulated the following assets:

Various IRA assets:	$350,000
401(K) assets:	$550,000
Personal Investments:	$600,000
Total Assets	$1,500,000

In addition, the Simpson's are contributing $14,000 annually into their 401(k) plan for the next three years.

They have received their social security statement and they expect to receive $22,000/year starting at age 66 (in four years). They have assumed a 2% inflation factor for both their retirement needs and their social security benefits.

They are planning on this retirement withdrawal till age 92 and do not intend to invade their principal.

They have gone to our web site www.larashullmay.com clicked Retirement Funding Analysis under online tools and completed the Retirement Funding Analysis

Their Retirement Funding analysis has calculated that they need to earn 6.64% on all their assets to achieve their retirement income goals. If you look in the Appendix you will see a printout of the Simpson's Retirement Funding Analysis.

Now look at the hypothetical goal sheet chart on the next page. It shows what their assets should be each quarter for the next several years. It also shows their performance for the quarter, year-to-date, and since inception.

By simply looking at the chart, the Simpson's can see whether they are behind or ahead of their goal. With just a quick glance they can see clearly that they are ahead of their target growth rate.

I encourage all of you reading this book to have your financial advisor provide you with a goal sheet so you can track your assets relative to your goals. If your advisor cannot provide you with a goal sheet relative to your goals send me an e-mail at ronl@larashullmay.com and I will be happy to send you the Excel template I have developed.

Prepared for Joe & Mary Simpson

Goals: 6.56% Yearly
 1.60% Quarterly

	Mar-04	Jun-04	Sep-04	Dec-04	Mar-05	Jun-05	Sep-05	Dec-05
Dain - Joe's Personal Account	500,000	508,245	530,458	540,034	533,004	548,715	566,217	578,986
Dain - Joint Account	246,851	265,187	268,485	266,006	281,198	297,995	306,162	305,426
Morningstar - Mary's IRA	75,011	76,154	73,156	80,245	81,345	82,456	85,126	85,865
Morningstar - Joe's SEP IRA	100,452	105,348	110,587	108,457	112,537	116,485	119,345	122,549
SubTotal	922,314	954,934	984,686	994,732	1,010,044	1,045,651	1,076,830	1,092,826
Net Deposits and Withdrawals								
Quarterly Performance (adjusted)		3.54%	3.12%	1.02%	1.54%	3.53%	2.98%	1.48%
Year to Date Performance (adjusted)		3.54%	6.76%	7.89%	1.54%	5.12%	8.26%	9.86%
Total Tracked Performance (adjusted)		3.54%	6.76%	7.89%	9.53%	13.37%	16.76%	18.49%

Quarterly Goal and Performance

Legend: Adjusted Goal Value; Actual Value

Chapter Seven

Your Probability
of Success

Now that you have completed the Retirement Funding Analysis you should have a better idea of the dollar amount and growth rate needed in order to achieve your retirement goals.

Do these numbers seem overwhelming or unachievable? Or are you comfortable with your ability to reach these important milestones? Either way, you must keep in mind that your success, in part, will depend upon market forces you (or I or anyone else) have no control over. Welcome to the world of investing!

I don't want to paint a bleak picture though. When it comes to investing, I believe the key to success is identifying a realistic return based on financial market history and then identifying investment vehicles that will allow you to achieve whatever benchmark you've set.

In fact, looking at the history of the markets is a good place to start when trying to figure out what your probability of success will be. For example, from 1930 to 2000, I looked at how the Dow performed every 10 years and found there were only three times in this 70-year period that it provided a return of 10 percent or better. This occurred in the 1950s, 1980s and 1990s – all time periods which were marked by steep declines in interest rates.

In all the other 10-year periods when interest rates were either flat or on the rise, the Dow gained an average of only 0.04 percent annually (that's right, it's not a typo). That's practically no gain at all for those 40 years. Eliminating the depression years of the 1930's the average annual gain for the 40's, 60's & 70's was only1.69%.

As I write this book in the summer of 2005, the Federal Reserve continues to raise short-term rates. If you combine this with the low value of the dollar compared to foreign currencies, surging oil and commodity prices and large budget deficits, the prospect for double digit returns over the next 10 years seems very unlikely.

On the brighter side, many corporations are flush with cash, corporate profits are increasing, productivity is improving, and worldwide competition is keeping inflation in check – all of which are good things for you and me and other investors. In short, these factors will be a positive for the equity markets. Nonetheless, double digit returns over the next 10 years shouldn't be expected, so you need to take this into account during your own planning.

The chart of the Dow Jones Industrial Averages for the past 100 years shows a pretty spectacular gain. However, from the year 1905, when the Dow stood at a low of 32.47, to the year 2005 and its high of 10,500, the annual growth rate is only 5.95%.

This period covers two world wars, the Korean & Vietnam Wars, Desert Storm and the Iraq War, presidential assassinations, the great depression and many other events that spooked the market.

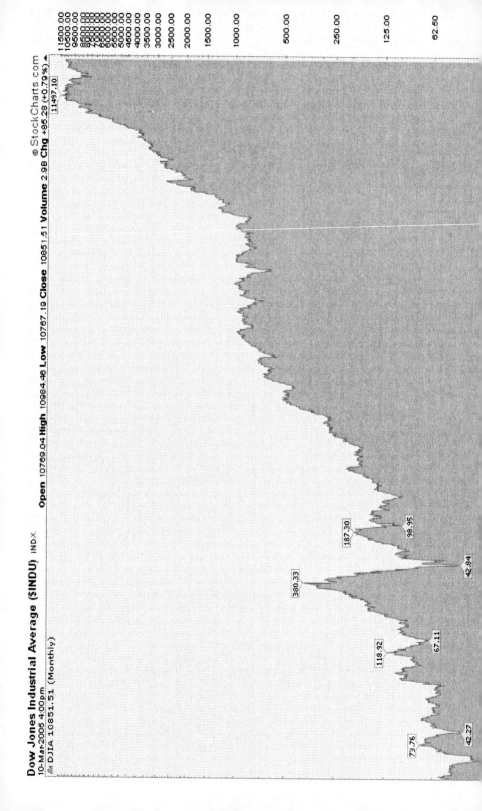

Clearly, you shouldn't base all of your investment strategy on the performance of the Dow stocks over a 100-year period. But given the size and importance of the Dow companies to the marketplace (they were picked as representative of the overall market for a reason), it does give you an idea of how difficult it can be to achieve anything over a 10 percent return.

Actually, the probability of achieving even a 7 – 8 percent return is pretty low given market history. While these rates are certainly attainable given the proper strategies and the right market conditions, there are still many factors, such as inflation and taxes, which can limit any returns your portfolio might create.

So where does this leave us? Well, I believe everyone (including myself) needs to find a way to achieve our retirement goals using a much lower growth rate. If after completing the Retirement Funding Analysis you discovered your situation requires a 7 – 15 percent annual return on your investments in order to achieve everything you want to do, you might want to go back and start to re-define and re-prioritize your goals. Why? Because I can almost guarantee that it would take an extraordinary situation for you to see this type of growth rate over a long period of time. Market history tells us this is the case even today.

Now, I'm not saying the "sky is falling," but I am trying to paint a realistic picture of what you should expect now and in the future. In fact, I believe we're currently entering a period of slowly rising interest rates over the next 10 – 15 years. And during this time, most analysts (including myself) foresee modest, single digit growth in corporate earnings, which will be negated by the slow rise in interest rates.

What does this mean? Simply put, all of this can have a significant impact on annual withdrawals from your retirement savings, and we face the possibility of having to do more with less.

If you recall, achieving high growth rates in the 1980s and 1990s wasn't much of a problem, especially when the market witnessed an explosion of fast-moving, highly-touted tech stocks. Today's market looks more like it did in the 1960s and 1970s when growth rates averaged only 2 - 3 percent.

To further demonstrate my point, let's take a look at a chart prepared by Metropolitan Life Insurance Company which shows the probability of an individual's retirement assets lasting for 20, 25 and 30 years based on different withdrawal rates AND different stock/bond investment mixes.

20-Year Retirement
Stock/Bond Investment Mix

Withdrawal Rate	100/0	80/20	60/40	40/60	15/85	5/95
4 %	96	98	99	99	99	99
5 %	90	92	95	97	99	98
6 %	78	81	82	81	69	48
7 %	64	63	57	44	12	1

As you can see in the graph above, there is a strong probability (more than 90 percent across the realm of possible stock/bond investment mixes) of your retirement assets lasting 20 years if only 5 percent is withdrawn each year. However, if the withdrawal rate needed is one percent higher (6 percent) then you will need a 60/40 stock/bond mixture of investments in order to reach the highest probability of success of 82%.

What happens if you need a 7 percent withdrawal rate each year? Well, this is where things get serious because the probability of achieving this withdrawal rate, even with an ideal 60/40 investment mix, is only **57** percent. Given this, you can see why it's very important to try to achieve your retirement objectives with a withdrawal rate of 5 percent or less.

But how does this change when looking at a 25- or 30-year retirement timeframe? Again, two charts produced by Metropolitan Life Insurance Company offer a look at what your probability of success will be for targeted withdrawal rates at different stock/bond investment mixes.

25-Year Retirement
Stock/Bond Investment Mix

Withdrawal Rate	100/0	80/20	60/40	40/60	15/85	5/95
4 %	92	94	97	98	99	99
5 %	81	83	83	80	69	42
6 %	66	65	61	43	14	1
7 %	48	43	33	12	0	0

30-Year Retirement
Stock/Bond Investment Mix

Withdrawal Rate	100/0	80/20	60/40	40/60	15/85	5/95
4 %	87	88	89	90	86	71
5 %	73	74	70	60	25	4
6 %	56	53	42	25	1	0
7 %	38	31	20	5	0	0

After reviewing the 25- and 30-year graphs, you can see some definite differences, especially when you start looking at how your probability of success is lowered as your retirement timeframe is lengthened.

For example, close examination of the 20- and 25-year tables shows a big difference between the probabilities of your retirement assets lasting the entire time if your withdrawal rate is 6 percent. For a 20-year timeframe, you have an 82 percent probability of your assets lasting with a 60/40 mix of investments. But this drops to 61 percent (using the same 60/40 mix) if the timeframe is increased to 25 years.

And if you really want a wake-up call, consider the figures shown in the 30-year table above. This chart alone strikes fear into the minds of individuals who thought their retirement assets would last forever!

Let's look at the probability of your retirement assets lasting 30 years. Using the same 60/40 mix, your probability of achieving a 6 percent withdrawal rate for the entire period is only 42 percent – as compared to 61 percent for 25 years and 82 percent for 20 years. How is this possible and what causes this to happen? Actually, it's pretty simple considering past history and well-documented market trends: Over a 30-year period you're bound to experience a substantial bear market, and a bear market is further exacerbated when you're withdrawing assets.

Bottom line, given the present market situation and the future outlook, the odds of achieving any growth rate in excess of 6 percent (let alone 7 percent) over a period of time is highly unlikely. So if this fits your situation, you need to start looking at how you will be taking your money out, as well as how and when you will be spending your money.

And the time to do this is now, especially if you haven't yet retired. Planning ahead and re-adjusting your goals and investment strategies will leave you in a much better position. Better than waiting, or doing nothing at all.

Everyone wants to be a success, right? Well, when it comes to your retirement and being able to "succeed" at all those things you want to do and experience, it's no different than any other pursuit you might undertake– you need to set goals, plan ahead and put some work into it in order to make it happen. Only then will your probability of success increase accordingly.

Tips You Can Use

Here's a suggestion regarding mortgages that can help to reduce the growth rate needed to achieve your retirement goal:

It might be a good idea to pay-off your mortgage. Why? Because if you've been paying on your mortgage for over 15 years the remaining balance will be quite low and the total monthly payments divided by your remaining mortgage will be quite high.

For example, say your original mortgage was $300,000 at 6 percent rate of interest. This means your monthly payment is approximately $1,800 per month. After 15 years, your mortgage balance will still be $213,146. However, if we add up your payments for twelve months we get approximately $21,600 (i.e. $1,800 x 12) in total annual payments. This represents a 10.13 percent return on the $213,146 remaining mortgage balance if you pay it off early. Tell me, where are you going to get a 10.13 percent return with any degree of safety?

Assuming an original 30-year mortgage of $300,000 at 6 percent, your monthly principal and interest payment is $1,798. The table below illustrates this point and shows the remaining balance and the percentage return you would have to earn if you were to invest your remaining mortgage balance.

$$1171 \times 12 = 14052$$

$$\frac{14,052}{212,000} = 6.63\%$$

Annual Payments as a Percentage of Mortgage Balance

Years Remaining on Mortgage	Remaining Balance	Annual Payments as % of Remaining Balance
29	296,315.96	7.28%
25	279,163.07	<u>7.73%</u>
20	251,057.17	8.60%
15	213,146.53	10.13%
14	204,105.57	10.57%
13	194,506.97	11.10%
12	184,316.36	11.71%
11	173,497.21	12.44%
10	162,010.76	13.32%
9	149,815.85	14.41%
8	136,868.78	15.77%
7	123,123.17	17.53%
6	108,529.76	19.89%
5	93,036.26	23.20%
4	76,587.16	28.18%
3	59,123.51	36.51%
2	40,582.73	53.18%
1	20,898.41	103.28%

Assumptions:

$300,000 original mortgage
6% mortgage interest rate
Monthly payment = $ 1,798
Annual Payments = $ 21,583

So, if you only have 10 years remaining on your mortgage, you should definitely pay it off, as it would take a 13.32 percent return on the $162,010 to equal your monthly payments. However, if you decide against paying-off your mortgage, consider refinancing it as an interest only loan, or a new 30-year mortgage to considerably lower your payment obligations.

Given all this, let me give you an idea of how the growth rate needed to achieve one's retirement income goals would be lowered if we paid-off the above $162,010 mortgage. If you assume that we are looking for $75,000 of spendable income, that we have $20,000 in social security benefits and $900,000 in IRA assets, that we are 65 years old and expect to live to age 92, the growth rate needed becomes 7.03 percent. However, if we pay-off the mortgage and subtract the $162,010 from our $900,000 in retirement assets, we now lower our retirement income needs from $75,000 annually to $53,400! This, in turn, lowers our growth rate to 5.36%. Needless to say, this is a significant outcome, as you would no longer have to take the risk of earning 7 percent (or more) per year. And because of this, you could then achieve all of your retirement goals by investing in U.S. government-guaranteed Ginnie Maes – which, again, is another significant development.

Don't believe me? I encourage you to go to our website (www.larashullmay.com), complete the Retirement Funding Analysis (RFA), and input the numbers I just gave you, which include a 2 percent consideration/assumption for inflation and Social Security benefits.

Chapter Eight

Should You Do This On Your Own?

One of the reasons our country is so great is that we, as citizens of the United States, have an amazing amount of freedom when it comes to how we make, manage and spend our money. Because of this, anyone preparing for retirement has a multitude of options when it comes to saving for it - stocks, bonds, IRAs, mutual funds, 401(K)s – to name but a few.

Furthermore, a society such as ours, overflowing with readily available information, makes it much easier to educate oneself on a wide variety of issues, including investing your money. Books, tapes, websites, magazines, seminars - you name it – are just a few examples of the sources out there for anyone interested in investing today. Some are good, some not so good, so a degree of caution is warranted as you tap into any of these resources, especially when employing the use of the Internet.

With all of these available resources, do I think people should undertake the monumental task of putting together and managing their own retirement portfolio? Unless you've had some type of professional training or education in investment strategies and/or tax planning, my answer is this: NO.

I believe the stakes are much too high for most everyone to go it alone down the "retirement investment road." And, unfortunately, many people are not as knowledgeable about investing as they think they are -an observation based on the experiences I've had with clients during my many years of providing financial planning counsel. In short, I can't tell you how many people I've worked with who realize their previously self-managed portfolios weren't doing as well as they should be.

Given this, I believe it's much better for individuals to have a financial advisor who not only has a professional investment background, but also knows how to incorporate tax planning strategies into the equation. Tax planning know-how is very important because being able to match your tax strategies with your investment strategies is key to getting the most mileage (and value) out of your retirement savings.

Having said this, it's important to remember that an educated investor – one who understands the basics of the market and has a solid grasp of his/her financial goals – is a financial planner's best client. So even if you do seek out and employ the services of a professional advisor, don't quit the learning process on your end. When it's time to work with your advisor, the more intelligently you can discuss your retirement goals and needs, as well as the investment vehicles to be used, the more comfortable you will feel about the steps to be taken down-the-road.

Some of you might be saying, "Why should I pay someone to help manage my retirement money when I'll probably need every penny of it to do what I want to do?" Employing the services of an experienced financial advisor will cost you some money, but I can also tell you the investment returns a good advisor produces will outpace anything you may have to pay for that advice. Additionally, a good advisor will help you stay-the-course and recommend sound adjustments to your portfolio based on market factors that could have a negative impact on your long-term savings.

With this in mind, I strongly recommend – if you haven't done so already – finding an experienced Certified Financial Planner (CFP) to help you in the process of managing and investing your retirement assets. Why? Well, below is an excellent example of how "doing it on your own" can lead to disaster.

Recently, I was referred to an individual – we'll call him "Charlie" – who had been the chief financial officer of a large company. Charlie had retired five years ago and felt he knew how to handle his investments. His attitude was: "No way am I going to pay a 1 percent asset management fee, and no way am I going to pay a CPA to give me professional tax advice or prepare my tax return." In addition, he didn't think it was important to pay an attorney to draft his will, let alone provide him with the estate planning strategies which could save his children over $2,000,000 in future estate taxes. Bottom line, Charlie knew it all and didn't want any help.

By the time I met Charlie he was in the fifth year of his "I'll do it myself" approach. And after encountering some serious setbacks, he was now searching for someone who could coordinate all of his tax and investment planning. In short, he had learned a lesson – the hard way.

Some of the errors, in my opinion, he had made solely on his own. For example, he had made a lucrative real estate investment that carried a 12% interest rate secured by real estate assets. However, he made it personally so he had to pay the federal and state income taxes on the 12% interest. If he had made the investment with his IRA assets, rather than his personal assets, he could have sheltered the 12 percent interest from ordinary income taxes. Real estate in an IRA? Yes, you can make real estate investments in an IRA. And if you have the right type of IRA that allows for alternative investments you can also invest in hard assets – like gold and silver, real estate, promissory notes. Keep in mind, I'm not recommending these as investments, but if you're an expert in any of these areas you should be aware that these options are available and offer you a way to invest in a personal area of expertise – which is something Charlie would have known if he'd consulted a financial planning professional from the start.

Charlie also had something I like to call "index sickness." He'd invested most of his assets in the S&P index, which, unfortunately, is made-up mostly of large cap stocks, some of which have not done well over the past five years. Furthermore, he hadn't properly asset allocated his assets to achieve the growth rate he needed. Given this, it also came as no surprise that Charlie didn't even know the growth rate he needed to earn to achieve his retirement goals.

Here's a brief overview of the damage Charlie had done to his own portfolio: He had withdrawn 5 percent of his assets from an index fund. Unfortunately, he started in January of 2000 and had not properly asset allocated his assets. Due to this, Charlie's assets, which originally totaled one million dollars, have declined to $556,294! So he has lost over 44 percent of his retirement assets, and the probability of achieving his retirement goals is now highly unlikely.

Look at the chart below:

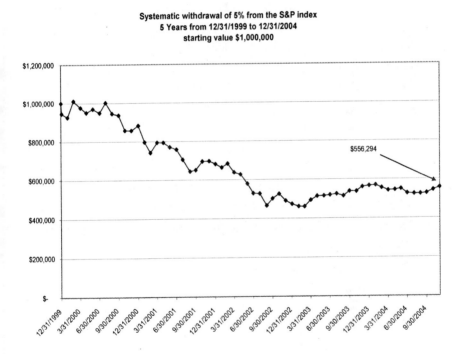

Systematic withdrawal of 5% from the S&P index
5 Years from 12/31/1999 to 12/31/2004
starting value $1,000,000

If Charlie had asset allocated his assets between the five asset classes outlined below, the final value of his account would have been $1,227,580 by December 31, 2004, even if he had withdrawn 5 percent annually. The lesson in all of this is simple: there's a big difference between losing over 40 percent of your retirement nest egg and having an additional 20 percent (or more) at the end of five years.

Investment	Initial Investment	Ending Value
S&P 500 – Large Cap Growth	$200,000	$119,205
Russell – Mid Cap Value	$200,000	$296,930
Dow Jones Real Estate	$200,000	$438,076
Lehman Bros Intmed Gov't.	$200,000	$216,013
Russell Top 200 Value	$200,000	$157,356
Total Investment	**$1,000,000**	**$1,227,580**

The above funds are index funds for their respective asset classes. The point is, if Charlie had asset allocated, he would have done extremely well – even in a negative market. This, my friends, is the whole point (and advantage) of asset allocation.

Tips You Can Use

If you plan on trying to "go it alone," you need to – at a minimum - subscribe to Morningstar. By doing so, you can research the various fund managers and rank them by performance in their respective asset classes. Keep in mind, though, you shouldn't look at just past performance. Why? Well, if the manager is a top manager in his/her asset class they will do well when that particular asset class does well.

Case in point: In December 1999, a former client of mine came to me complaining about the horrible performance of his real estate mutual funds and the poor performance of his mid-cap value managers. After doing so, he pulled his account and went into large cap growth stocks – primarily tech-related stocks – on his own. Yes, real estate did poorly in 1998 and 1999, but REIT funds averaged over 20 percent a year from January 2000 to December 2004; and value stocks, which did poorly in 1998 and 1999, have done extremely well over the past five years. Given this, it doesn't take much to guess what has probably happened to this person's money, at least what's left of it.

The lesson is this: You don't know which asset class will do well, so it's important to be diversified by asset class. I know this advice sounds like a song coming from a broken record, but if this is the only thing you get out of this book I'll be happy. And so will you, in the long run.

E. Ronald Lara, CFP

Chapter Nine

What to Look For in a Financial Advisor

My wife is always reminding me, "You get what you pay for." And this certainly holds true when it comes to finding the right financial advisor to help you with the important task of managing your retirement funds.

Keep in mind, this doesn't mean the most expensive advisor will give you the best advice and get you the best returns. What's more important is finding an advisor who shares your investment philosophy and operates on the same wavelength that you do. In short, your advisor needs to be someone you can connect with and respect. This alone will go a long way toward building a trusting and beneficial relationship, one that can help you reach your retirement goals.

How do you find someone like this? Well, many of my clients are referred to me by their own friends, family and/or business acquaintances – all of whom have had good experiences with our firm and the services we offer. Given this, I'd recommend that you ask your own friends and family for names of professional financial advisors they might know. If they can't point you in the right direction, there are some easily accessible resources you can tap into for current information on credible, experienced advisors in your area. Remember, the financial services industry is one of the most highly regulated industries on the planet, so there is a wealth of information available to consumers regarding the firms and/or individuals they use to help them with investments and retirement planning.

One great place to start is the Financial Planning Association (FPA) in Denver, Colorado. As a professional association, they offer a referral service and can also provide great background information on the industry as a whole. Any reputable financial planner or advisor is going to belong to this group. You can reach them at www.fpanet.org.

Once you've identified a possible financial planner – whether it's through a referral and/or by way of the FPA - another good place to look for background information is the National Association of Securities Dealers (NASD) at www.nasd.com. This is an important resource because it's here you can verify a planner's history, as well as find out if any disciplinary actions have been taken against them.

Prior actions against a financial planner should always be taken into consideration before using their services. If, in fact, you do discover some type of action has been taken against them, make sure you ask about this – it's something the planner should be able to address and explain with complete honesty. Any planner or advisor with multiple violations should probably be avoided, and by all means stay away from anyone who has been disciplined for "unauthorized transactions."

I also believe it's important to hire a financial planner who utilizes asset allocation software as a part of their services. If they have this, they should be able to tell you how much to invest in each asset class in order to achieve your desired growth rate with the least amount of risk. In addition, a good financial advisor should also be able to provide you information about themselves and their practice, as well as offer you reports on the managers of all the funds they invest in on behalf of their clients.

You will be doing yourself a big favor by conducting your own due diligence and thoroughly checking out a financial planner before employing them to help you with your retirement portfolio. Remember to ask them questions, ask for references and, by all means, check-up on them with the tools you have available via the Internet and professional associations.

A good example of why asking questions and checking references is so important is illustrated by an individual I met several years ago who had approximately $700,000 to invest. He told me how a so-called financial planner had recommended that he invest in the Kingdom Fund which GUARANTEED a 2 percent return PER MONTH! (Folks, the only guarantees I'm counting on in life are death, taxes, and U.S. Treasury Bills - if you hold them to maturity, of course).

Needless to say, this individual had not been given a copy of the "planner's" ADV Part II (more on that later); didn't see a S.I.P.C. plaque in the office; and thought it all sounded too good to be true. To his credit, he furnished me with the information and I passed it on to the Securities and Exchange Commission (SEC) office in Philadelphia. Several months later the SEC brought enforcement action against several individuals involved with this ponzi scheme.

Bottom line, it's ultimately up to you – the investor – to be the biggest, most vocal, protector of your money. Why? Well, it's YOUR money and it's YOUR livelihood and retirement at stake. Given this, you should do whatever you can in your power to safeguard these hard-earned dollars. If it means educating yourself about investing – then do it. If it means asking a lot of questions and demanding satisfactory answers – then do it. If it means interviewing more than one financial planner until you find someone you like and feel comfortable with – then do it. Why? Because if you don't, no one else will!

Tips You Can Use

Whether you're starting a new account or transferring existing accounts, here are a few questions you should ask any Certified Financial Planner before putting your money in their care:

Question: **How will you determine what investments are best for me and my situation?**

Comments: They should tell you a retirement funding analysis of your needs will be done to determine the growth rate needed to achieve your goals. Once this is completed, your funds should be asset allocated to achieve your goals.

Question: **What are your fees?**

Comments: Remember, you get what you pay for, so getting financial planning advice (and related services) for free isn't necessarily a good goal. Paying 1 – 1.5 percent of assets under management is a reasonable fee, but if you just require the purchase of U.S. Treasury Bonds, or mortgage-backed bonds, they might do that on a commission basis rather than a fee basis. Some planners use C Share mutual funds in which you don't pay a fee, but the planner receives .80 - 1.00 percent from the mutual fund as a 12(b)-1 fee. This is usually more economical if the planner is recommending several mutual funds, along with individual bonds, so you're not paying a fee for the planner to hold the bonds.

Question: **Can I have a copy of your ADV Part II?**

Comments: You should DEFINITELY receive this before you leave their office. It's required by the planner to provide this to you. In short, it will explain a lot about their practice and list any disciplinary action taken against them from a regulatory agency, such as the NASD, SEC or any state government securities and/or insurance commissioners.

Question: Can I have the names and numbers of one or two of your clients for a reference call?

Comments: A planner should jump at the chance to provide you with the names of his clients. They will likely refer you to their better clients, but you can learn a lot about your future financial planner by speaking to them – especially if you were not referred to this planner from an existing client.

Question: Who will hold my securities?

Comments: Most planners have a clearing firm to hold clients' assets, with the large brokerage firms usually holding their own. Some individuals prefer to have a "name" firm, such as Merrill Lynch or Morgan Stanley, hold their assets because they know they're not going to go out of business. But for the most personalized, hands-on professional service, I'd recommend looking for a certified financial planner in a smaller, independent firm.

Question: Can I see your S.I.P.C. plaque?

Comments: By having this on display, it simply means their broker/dealer is insured by the Securities Investor Protection Corporation (S.I.P.C.). This doesn't protect your account against losses, but it does insure you if the brokerage firm goes under.

Question: **How often will I get performance reports for my accounts?**

Comments: At a minimum, you should receive these every quarter, but the information should be available to you anytime upon request.

Question: **What happens if my account declines?**

Comments: Your account will likely go down (or lose value) some quarters, so you must be prepared for this. However, your declines will be minimal and your long-term progress will be smoother if your funds are properly asset allocated. Given this, the planner should explain the process of rebalancing your portfolio (especially in a declining market), which should be done at least annually. Don't switch advisors just because your account declines in value. If you are properly asset allocated your account should not decline as much as the averages. In addition, if you have top quartile managers your account should recover quickly as the market rebounds.

Question: I've heard of an Investment Policy Statement. What exactly is an IPS?

Comments: An Investment Policy Statement offers guidelines for: 1) determining the growth rate you need to achieve; 2) establishing the time frame needed to achieve your goals; and 3) detailing your investment plan's asset allocation. If you don't receive an IPS how do you know what the advisor's objectives are? Consider switching advisors if you are not offered an IPS.

Question: **What fees will I have to pay if I decide to pull my account?**

Comments: You should have very few fees to pay if you decide to change planners. Most likely, you will pay a prorated quarterly fee, or a few commissions to sell securities if you want to transfer cash. However, if you're changing firms I recommend you transfer your assets in-kind. This will eliminate the temptation for your present planner/broker to charge you a high commission for selling your securities. Also, your new planner will charge you little, if any, commissions to liquidate your previous holdings to re-asset allocate those assets into his/her recommendations.

Question: **How important is honesty and integrity to you?**

Comments: While most individuals in the financial planning service industry uphold a high degree of honesty and integrity, there are a few who will take advantage of your ignorance. Don't hesitate to contact the NASD if you suspect dishonesty (of any type) has taken place. However, I would first contact the planner's supervisor (if there is one) before you contact the NASD, as a more immediate response to your complaint(s) would likely come from them.

Chapter Ten

Investment Product Overview

As I've already outlined in earlier chapters, there are a number of different ways you can invest your retirement savings. However, it's important to keep in mind that how you asset allocate your retirement portfolio to achieve the growth rate needed to successfully realize your retirement income objectives is critical to your overall success.

I say this because not all investment opportunities offer the returns and/or performance over the long-term you will need in order to meet your retirement goals. Given this, it's important you educate yourself on what certain investment vehicles can, and cannot, do. Doing this will better prepare you for conversations with your financial advisor, as well as help you better determine what kinds of investments you're most comfortable with in terms of risks and possible returns.

Or think of it this way: Your investments will be some of the biggest purchases made during your lifetime. For example, before buying a home you find out as much as you can about the house you're interested in, and you visit it a few times before making a decision. The same goes for buying a car – you do your research, test drive it, and even ask others what they think about it. My point is this: You need to take the same care and do the same research and fact-finding when deciding where to invest money in your retirement portfolio.

Keeping all this in mind, here are a number of investment options and strategies you might want to consider for your retirement portfolio:

1. I strongly recommend an asset allocated portfolio of different asset classes. This can easily be achieved by using mutual funds which are managed for a specific asset class. For example, if you need a portion of your portfolio to be in international stocks, it's much easier to invest in a mutual fund whose primary objective is international growth, as opposed to investing in individual international companies. You could select a private manager to do this for you if your portfolio is over $1,000,000, but you can also select an excellent international mutual fund on your own if you do your homework.

2. Consider using the services of a Certified Financial Planner who uses an asset allocation software program. There are several reputable companies that offer this service. Your portfolio will include 10 – 15 top managers who are constantly supervising and rebalancing in response to market fluctuations. I personally have an IRA

account in excess of $1,000,000 managed by a leading mutual fund research firm.

3. If the growth rate needed to achieve your retirement objective is less than 7 percent, you will probably have a portion of it in fixed income investments. If this is the case, be sure to utilize Ginnie Mae, Fannie Mae and Freddie Mac mortgage-backed bonds to provide you with a monthly interest check. These mortgage-backed bonds, which usually yield between 5.0 - 5.5 percent (or higher), are rated AAA; and Ginnie Maes are backed by the full faith and credit of the U.S. government.

4. If you need to have a portion of your assets in short-term maturities, please use short-term U.S. Treasury Bonds! Despite their obvious advantages, I rarely meet a new client who has invested in them. One-year Treasury Notes currently yield in excess of 3 percent and are exempt from state income taxes. Thus, a 3 percent Treasury yield is equivalent to 3.2 percent for a resident in a state with a 6 percent state income tax. For a slightly higher yield, your advisor should be able to offer you competitive certificates of deposits from a number of banks.

5. It's also important to have a portion of your fixed income portfolio in international bonds to act

as a hedge against a falling dollar on international markets.

6. With the prospect of rising commodity prices – due to the demand from markets in China, India and other developing nations – a natural resource fund would be appropriate in a portfolio where the growth rate needed is in excess of 6 percent.

7. While I'm not a big fan of variable annuities, there is legislation being proposed that would make the first $20,000 of annuity income from an IRA tax free. This could be significant if you're in the top tax bracket and could save you as much as $8,000 per year in income taxes! However, to qualify for this you must annuitize your annuity. Why? The government doesn't want you running out of money; so by annuitizing a portion of your assets you will be guaranteed the monthly income for as long as you live.

8. Once you have selected several mutual fund managers to invest with, preferably with the guidance of a Certified Financial Planner, you can check their performance relative to other asset managers in their respective class. Hopefully, they will all be top quartile managers. There's really no reason why you should place your investments in the care of anyone but the best. Right?

9. Stick with quality. Philip Carret, who founded the Pioneer Fund in 1927, gave me some advice

which I have never forgotten. He said more people lose money going after a little more yield than for any other reason. Stick with quality bonds. Don't buy individual BBB rated bonds or lower. Invest in AAA mortgage backed bonds from the Federal Home Loan Administration (Freddie Mac), Federal National Mortgage Association (Fannie Mae) or, better still, the Government Mortgage Association (Ginnie Mae).

10. Finally, make sure your investment advisor gives you an Investment Policy Statement (IPS) that clearly lays out the objectives you are trying to achieve, the time horizon, the asset allocation and, most importantly, the growth rate you are trying to achieve.

E. Ronald Lara, CFP

Chapter Eleven

Conclusion:
Making It All Work For You

As I've tried to demonstrate throughout this book, there are many important things to consider when investing for retirement. The key is to find a way to separate the good information from the bad and use this knowledge to your advantage. Hopefully, it will boost your retirement portfolio in the process.

If you look around today, you can see we're bombarded by all kinds of information regarding investment opportunities. Magazines tell us about "hot stocks;" print ads tout "great investment opportunities;" a plethora of websites provide instant access to all sorts of real-time information about where we should put our money. Even cable television offers programs with "experts" giving anyone watching a firsthand look at what's happening in the markets on a minute-by-minute basis. Put all these together with the hundreds of investment-related books on the market today and you can see how it can become a confusing mix to sort through.

I'll be the first to tell you there are plenty of dangers out there when it comes to finding good places to invest your money. But I can also honestly say I've never seen anyone lose money in the market after using a well-diversified portfolio for 10 years or more. This is possible because they have successfully separated marketing messages from reality and found a way to effectively distribute their hard-earned dollars amongst a host of credible, well-established investment opportunities (most often with the help of a good advisor).

For this reason, I cannot reiterate too often how important asset allocation is to the long-term health (and growth) of your retirement portfolio. Bottom line, this is one of your most important keys to success, but it's a process that must be regularly monitored in order to maximize your returns over the long run. In addition to evaluating your managers each year you should also rebalance your portfolio to its original percentage allocation.

Here's how re-balancing your assets works: Certain managers will have appreciated in value while some may have declined in value over the past year. The managers that have appreciated in value now have a greater percentage of your portfolio assets. By selling assets from the appreciated managers and reinvesting in the managers that have declined, you will restore your portfolio to its original asset allocation balance – the one that is designed to achieve the growth rate needed to realize your retirement goals. Re-balancing has been shown to add between 1.5 – 2.0% annually to a portfolio.

Fortunately, I've found that many people understand the importance of asset allocation in order to avoid the danger of "putting all their eggs (i.e. money) in one basket." However, despite the asset allocating many people employ, I have yet to meet someone who has re-balanced their portfolio on their own. In fact, this is a step most people avoid altogether and will only do after we've reviewed its importance.

So when it comes to figuring out your best course of action regarding asset allocation and/or re-balancing your portfolio, there's no better way to do this than to enlist the help of a qualified and trusted financial advisor. Even I – an experienced financial planner – tap into the knowledge of other professionals to manage my money. In fact, I currently have a leading asset allocation financial service firm managing 90 percent of my own retirement portfolio because they manage money through a time-tested approach of asset allocation. So if this is something I do, doesn't it make sense you should do it as well?

Bottom line, you owe it to yourself to do something – and to do it now. Why? Because waiting to take the important steps I've outlined in this book can cost you money in the long-run – money you could be using to achieve your retirement goals and dreams.

So start now and, by all means, enjoy your retirement!

E. Ronald Lara, CFP

Resources

Listed below are web sites that can provide useful information:

www.larashullmay.com our firm's web site has several online tools you will find useful. Our main online tool is the Retirement Funding Analysis that determines the growth rate you need to achieve your retirement income goal. In addition we have a minimum distribution calculator, education funding analysis and other tools you will find of interest.

www.financeyahoo.com this is a great web site to track all your security holdings if your current investment firm doesn't provide you with internet access.

www.closedendfund.com excellent site to find information regarding information on various closed end funds. Lists discount to net asset values and much more.

www.fpanet.org Financial Planning Association (FPA) – good place to search for a Certified Financial Planner CFP

www.nasd.com National Association of Securities Dealers – they regulate all the stock brokers. Great site to find any disciplinary history on your advisor or broker

The Retirement Funding Analysis for Joe Simpson, our fictitious client discussed in chapter 6, follows on the next five pages.

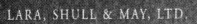

LARA, SHULL & MAY, LTD.

THE RETIREMENT FUNDING ANALYSIS

PREPARED FOR Joe & Mary Simpson

PREPARED BY E. Ronald Lara CFP

GENERAL INFORMATION

BIRTHDATE 12/15/1943   AGE YOU PLAN TO RETIRE 65

ANNUAL RETIREMENT INCOME DESIRED (today's dollars, before tax) $120,000

RETIREMENT ASSETS AT DEATH (Assets to leave your heirs) $1,501,000

RETIREMENT INCOME INFLATION RATE (% increase of Annual Income desired) 2.0%

LIFE EXPECTANCY AGE 92

CURRENT TAX BRACKET

FEDERAL % 33   STATE % 6

RETIREMENT ASSETS

STOCK OPTIONS VALUE $ 0

CURRENT RETIREMENT ASSETS $ 600,000
(401k, IRA, SEP, Pension and profit sharing assets, etc.)

LARA, SHULL & MAY, LTD.

RETIREMENT ASSETS (CONT.)

ANNUAL RETIREMENT CONTRIBUTIONS (Individual and employer contributions) $ 14,000

INDIVIDUAL ASSETS (Liquid assets to be used for retirement, not including $ 600,000
personal residence or other non-liquid assets)

ANNUAL SAVINGS (Amount deposited into savings plan per year) $0

DEFERRED COMPENSATION BALANCE TO DATE $0

ANNUAL DEFERRED COMPENSATION CONTRIBUTIONS $0

RETIREMENT INCOME SOURCES

ANNUAL PENSION INCOME AT RETIREMENT $0

ANNUAL SOCIAL SECURITY INCOME $ 22,000

DEFERRED COMPENSATION ANNUAL INCOME $0

AGE DEFERRED COMPENSATION BENEFITS END 92

ANNUAL OTHER INCOME 1 (Rental, royalty income etc.) $0

ANNUAL OTHER INCOME 2 $0

COST OF LIVING ADJUSTMENTS

SOCIAL SECURITY COLI (Cost of living adjustments) 2.0%

PENSION COLI (Cost of living increase, annually) $0

LARA, SHULL & MAY, LTD.

THE RETIREMENT FUNDING ANALYSIS

Based on the information you provided, the growth rate needed to achieve your retirement goals is 6.64%

See below for your projected retirement assets, per year, based on your calculated investment growth rate and savings rate.

It has been shown that asset allocation—not market timing or stock selection—is the primary determinant of variation in portfolio performance. Most individuals take on too much risk in their investments and thus fail to achieve their goals. In the current economic climate, it is especially important to have the correct asset allocation.

We would like to help you achieve your retirement planning goals. Please contact us for the proper asset allocation based on the above growth rate and your risk tolerance.

PRE-RETIREMENT ACCUMULATION

Age	Annual Contributions	Projected Assets
63	$ 14,000	$1,613,600
64	$ 14,000	$1,734,743
65	$ 14,000	$1,863,930

The above is by no means a guarantee of future performance. Actual results will vary.

8000 Towers Crescent Drive • Suite 660 • Vienna • Virginia 22182-2700
phone 703.827.2300 • fax 703.827.2314 • toll free 1.800.842.8834 • www.larashullmay.com

RETIREMENT YEARS

Age	Retirement Income Desired	SS Pension Benefits	Deferred Comp. Other Income	Shortfall	Remaining Retirement Assets
66	$129,753	$23,788	$0	$105,965	$1,881,730
67	$132,348	$24,264	$0	$108,084	$1,898,593
68	$134,995	$24,749	$0	$110,246	$1,914,414
69	$137,695	$25,244	$0	$112,451	$1,929,080
70	$140,449	$25,749	$0	$114,700	$1,942,471
71	$143,258	$26,264	$0	$116,994	$1,954,457
72	$146,123	$26,789	$0	$119,334	$1,964,900
73	$149,045	$27,325	$0	$121,720	$1,973,649
74	$152,026	$27,871	$0	$124,155	$1,980,545
75	$155,067	$28,429	$0	$126,638	$1,985,415
76	$158,168	$28,997	$0	$129,171	$1,988,076
77	$161,331	$29,577	$0	$131,754	$1,988,330
78	$164,558	$30,169	$0	$134,389	$1,985,966
79	$167,849	$30,772	$0	$137,077	$1,980,758
80	$171,206	$31,388	$0	$139,818	$1,972,462
81	$174,630	$32,016	$0	$142,615	$1,960,818
82	$178,123	$32,656	$0	$145,467	$1,945,550
83	$181,658	$33,309	$0	$148,376	$1,926,358
84	$185,319	$33,975	$0	$151,344	$1,902,924
85	$189,025	$34,655	$0	$154,371	$1,874,908
86	$192,806	$35,348	$0	$157,458	$1,841,943
87	$196,662	$36,055	$0	$160,607	$1,803,641
88	$200,595	$36,776	$0	$163,819	$1,759,583
89	$204,607	$37,511	$0	$167,096	$1,709,324

RETIREMENT YEARS

Age	Retirement Income Desired	SS Pension Benefits	Deferred Comp. Other Income	Shortfall	Remaining Retirement Assets
90	$208,699	$38,262	$0	$170,438	$1,652,385
91	$212,873	$39,027	$0	$173,847	$1,588,257
92	$217,131	$39,807	$0	$177,323	$1,516,394

Ron Lara is available for speaking engagements and personal appearances. For more information contact Ron at:

VIRGINIA OFFICE
Lara, Shull & May, Ltd.
8000 Towers Crescent Drive
Suite 660
Vienna, VA 22182-2700
Phone: 703-827-2300
Toll Free:800-842-8834

COLORADO OFFICE
Lara, Shull & May, Ltd
PO Box 2744
Frisco, CO 80443

Phone: 970-668-5700
Toll Free:877-543-5444

E-mail: ronl@larashullmay.com

To order additional copies of this book or to see a complete list of all **ADVANTAGE BOOKS™** visit our online bookstore at: www.advbookstore.com or call our toll free order number at: 1-888-383-3110

Advantage
BOOKS

Longwood, Florida, USA

"we bring dreams to life"™
www.advbooks.com

Printed in the United States
49343LVS00003B/49-96